JOURNEY

to

𝔟𝔶

OPRAH WINFREY

PHOTOGRAPHS BY
KEN REGAN

HYPERION
𝔑𝔢𝔴 𝔜𝔬𝔯𝔨

1998.

JOURNEY

to

by

OPRAH WINFREY

PHOTOGRAPHS BY
KEN REGAN

HYPERION
New York

1998.

BELOVED

𝕳𝖞𝖕𝖊𝖗𝖎𝖔𝖓
114 FIFTH AVENUE, NEW YORK, NY 10011.

Library of Congress Cataloging-in-Publication Data

Winfrey, Oprah.
    Journey to Beloved / by Oprah Winfrey : photographs by Ken Regan.
  --1st ed.
      p.   cm.
    ISBN 0-7868-6458-3
    1. Beloved (Motion picture : 1998) I. Title.
  PN1997.B276w56   1998
    791.43'72--DC21   98-26255
                                                          CIP

FIRST EDITION
10   9   8   7   6   5   4   3   2   1

DESIGNED BY NUMBER 17, NEW YORK.

PRINTED IN THE UNITED STATES OF AMERICA

FOR ALL THE ANCESTORS

whose lives

were a bridge

to this moment

My original intention in making BELOVED was the same as Toni Morrison's intention in writing the book: I wanted people to be able to feel deeply on a very personal level what it meant to be a slave, what slavery did to a people, and also to be liberated by that knowledge. I never felt so free and so joyful as when I was working on BELOVED.

Oprah Winfrey

JOURNEY TO

BELOVED

THE
FOREWORD

or

AN ESSAY BY

JONATHAN DEMME

my hero

THE
FOREWORD

of

AN ESSAY BY

JONATHAN DEMME

my hero

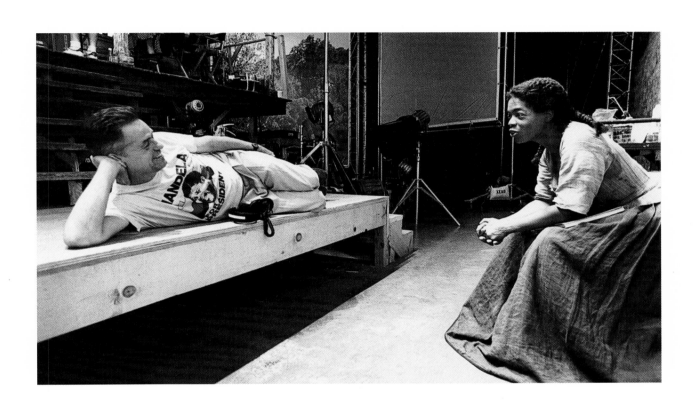

The day the script of BELOVED *arrived from Oprah's office I read it and was tremendously moved. It dealt with subject matter and themes — including this country's legacy of slavery — that I'd been wanting to work with for years. The characters had such amazing depth. And even though it would be a movie set in the post–Civil War period, I felt it would have extraordinary resonance for us today.*

❡Oprah Winfrey is so well known and dearly loved as a Major Public Figure *that when I originally put the script down, I wasn't sure whether her real-life cultural persona could be overcome — if "suspension of disbelief" could be achieved — in her playing Sethe on-screen. But my doubts were dispelled as soon as I heard Oprah*

speak of her passion for BELOVED at our first meeting. Her vision of Sethe filled me with such excitement and inspiration that I leapt, on the spot, to the belief that Oprah had been born to play this part.

¶While watching the movie, I find myself sometimes literally searching Sethe's face for the Oprah Winfrey we all know so vividly as the Major Public Figure, and I can't find her there.

¶True, Oprah underwent significant physical changes as she created Sethe. She literally reshaped herself; the hairstyles that were chosen have nothing to do with the look we know so well. But it's not simply the physical change that makes the transformation so utterly complete, natural, and profound. After all, physical-side alterations are often what the movies are all about.

¶It's deeper than that. Oprah had explained to me when we originally met that it was her goal and intention to channel the spirit of Margaret Garner, the woman whose cataclysmic real-life experience had first given birth to the idea for Beloved in the mind of Toni Morrison. This very infusion of humanity past accounts to a significant degree for Oprah's stunning alchemy, her astonishing abandonment of self in her BELOVED performance.

¶Oprah's biggest challenge in the making of BELOVED was the need for her to completely liberate herself from her own compassion for Sethe and Margaret Garner. Oprah—the incredibly deeply feeling person that she is—might have had the impulse to weep for Sethe. But Sethe, except under very particular

circumstances, never weeps for herself. That is almost her point.

¶Toni Morrison has said that it's imperative to look back at our country's tortured racial past without blinking. I'm thrilled at the way BELOVED *looks back from the strife-torn America of today. One of the great achievements of the book is in making it possible for the reader to encounter emotionally and consider that past, and the movie is an attempt to capture that goal on film.*

¶People sometimes ask Toni Morrison, "Why tell this excruciating story?" I've heard her reply that however heartbreaking and even conflicting it is to focus on Sethe's ordeal, this story also bears witness to the monumental truth that the slaveowners didn't win.

¶How does a mother show her greatest love for her children? Which is the most damning choice for a mother: to return her child to slavery or to spare the child slavery by taking its life?

¶Encountering this question on film, making the movie BELOVED, *joining up with Oprah Winfrey and Beah Richards, Danny Glover, Kimberly Elise, Thandie Newton, Lisa Gay Hamilton, Albert Hall, and the rest of our extraordinary cast and crew, was one of the most deepening and emotionally transcendent experiences of my life. What a blessing and awesome opportunity I was given to work with Oprah and that book and that cast and to try with my collaborators to make* BELOVED—*the* movie—*have a life all its own.*

Jonathan Demme   *April 24, 1998*

THE
STORY

or

HOW I FEEL ABOUT

BELOVED

[the book, the movie,
and the whole experience]

THE
STORY

of

HOW I FEEL ABOUT

BELOVED

[the book, the movie,
and the whole experience]

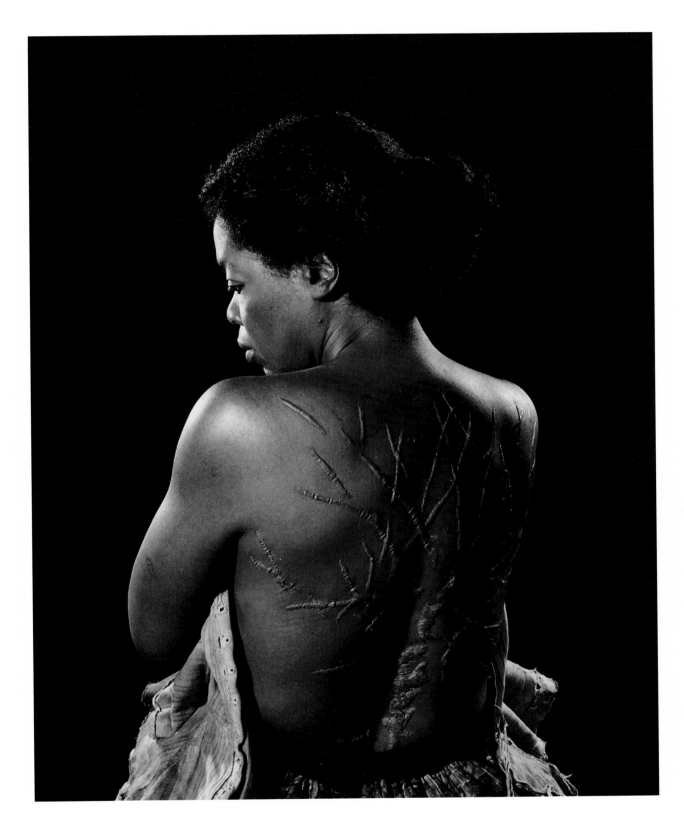

PART ONE.

I first read Toni Morrison's Beloved *when it came out*

in 1987. Started to read it and stopped, read it and stopped. But as with all of Toni Morrison's books, you need to give yourself time. I realized I wasn't going to get the essence of the story if I continued to go about it that way. So I made an appointment with myself to read the book. I got up on a Saturday morning and read from 7 until 4:30 in the afternoon, when I finished it.

I was taken in. The book took me in. I felt absorbed by it. I felt I was in the interior of the words. The words resonated with me in a way that doesn't often happen. There's a difference between reading a book and enjoying—even loving—the story, and having the feeling that the words are somehow connect-  ed to some part of you, and that then becomes your story. I felt in some way it was my own re-membering. I knew it, I knew Sethe, when I encoun-tered her I felt that she was in some way a part of my-self. I didn't know how and wasn't able to explain who this woman was and why it felt so much like myself. But I felt that I knew her or had known her or was in some way connected to her. And the more I read, the deeper that feel-ing became, and I was overcome with the idea of bringing her to life.

My first notion was to find Toni Morrison that very day so that I could get the film rights to the book, and I spent the rest of the after-noon trying to get her number. If it had been a weekday I could have called the publisher. Instead, I tried calling people who I thought would have her number—and they didn't. In the back of the book it mentioned the town she lived in, and I ended up calling the fire depart-ment, asking them to please go to their little blue reference book that tells the streets every-one lives on in the town, and could they please call Toni Morrison up and say to her that I was trying to reach her. And they did; they called me back, gave me the number, and I telephoned her that evening. I told her I'd just read the book (I think I was crying at first) and what it meant to me and how I felt so strongly that the world needed to hear this story, and the way to do it was through film. And she laughed and said, "How can you be serious? How could this ever be a movie?" And I was saying, I believe I can do it, I know how to do it. I didn't *really* know how, though I trusted the way would be provided for me.

When I was young I put myself through school being an orator, speaking at black churches and community organizations. And I remember when I was 22 speaking at the Union Baptist Church in Nashville, just before I moved to Baltimore, and I was doing the Sunday sermon; I had been invited to be the guest speaker. I was in the pulpit and remember say-ing to the crowd: I don't know what the future holds for me, but I know who holds the future.

I have always had faith that my life will be fine and there is a bigger picture in store for me that I can't even imagine for myself. I have since come to know that God can dream a bigger dream for you (for me) than you can dream for yourself, and that the whole role for your life on Earth is to attach yourself to that divine force and let yourself be released to it. And I felt the same way about making a movie of *Beloved.* Somehow I felt it was divine—I don't know what other word to use. Didn't know how, didn't care how long it would take. But felt it was meant to be.

So Toni Morrison said, "Okay, let's talk about it." I said I'd have someone call her on Monday. Then I told my attorney, whatever she asks for, give it to her. I don't want negotiations or to get lawyers involved. Whatever she wants, let's just sign the check. And he said, "That's not the way it's done." But I said that's the way this will be done. I signed the check and was thrilled to do so. The day I signed it was one of the happiest days of my life.

What I love about the story of Beloved is that it allows you to *feel* what slavery was like; it doesn't just intellectually *show* you the picture. It puts a human face on it and makes it so personal you feel the pain. When I finished reading the book I felt I'd been into the interior of what it is like to have endured and come out of slavery. It's not just about whippings or beatings or what was done to us; it's also about people who had experienced slavery in their uniqueness and individuality. You know, a lot of people went insane. The very idea of someone repressing your ability to think and have free will—if that wouldn't make you insane, then nothing would. And what I took from this experience was that if slavery didn't make you insane, then nothing ever should. If you are a descendant of slaves in this country, then nothing should ever make you crazy because you've already come through that. The one ultimate gift that God gives you is free will, the ability to think and to have your thoughts mean something. Everything in existence begins with thought. You create your life based upon what you think. You think and act upon your thoughts. If you don't have that, then you're not functioning as a human. And that's what slavery does: It makes you inhuman. It's the most inhumane practice on earth. It's not what God would bestow upon people.

I was raised in the Baptist Church, I grew up singing, "And before I'll be a slave/I'll be buried in my grave/And go home to my Lord and be free." I used to sing that hymn, but I didn't know its meaning until I did this movie. They were just words, and it was a nice, beautiful song . . . and you'd think, *Oh, my, what black people have come through!* Now I know it in the depths of my being: I will be buried and will bury my children with me before I will let you take me. I will not let you have me, because my will is that I belong to myself. The plan was that Sethe was going to kill all her children, then kill herself in order to get all of them to the other side. And that was her song. I remember I was getting ready to do a scene for the film, and singing that song to myself, just pacing back and forth—and that's when it hit me. And I started to weep.

Does Sethe have free will? As a slave on the Sweet Home plantation she doesn't, but once she's free, absolutely. Even when she kills her child when "schoolteacher" (enslaver) was coming to get her. People resented Sethe not because of what she did but because there was never a moment of regret. She didn't crumble, she didn't fall. She had 28 days of freedom, waking up in the morning deciding for herself what to do for the day—"hearing my boys laugh a laugh . . . First I get scared, then I realized if they laughed that hard all day, be the only hurt they have"—28 days of seeing what free colored people looked like for the first time. That spirit of community and friendship . . . 28 days of freedom, not 2, not 12 (they say it takes 21 days for a practice to become a habit): just enough to feel it, just enough to relax and believe that this is the way life can be.

I don't know what I would have done faced with Sethe's choice. With the personality I have created based on my current life experience, I probably would have tried to find "some other way," as Paul D admonished her, to survive. What I admired and what resonated with me was her strength, her iron-will refusal not to be taken down or taken back.

There are those who will argue that Sethe didn't have the right to make the choice for her children. I cannot judge her. She thought she was going to the other side, someplace that was a better place than a world where they milked you like a cow and treated you like an animal . . . or less than an animal. She's a mother making a choice for what she believes is right for her children. Because she has seen slavery. As far as Sethe is concerned, there is no choice between death in life — the daily death of slavery —

and some existence on the other side that promises redemption.

Now, Beloved is a baby and doesn't understand all of this. Sethe's relationship with Beloved is as crazy as one can get. It's confused, and the love is so thick, but Sethe can't explain it. You can never explain to someone, "I loved you so much I had to kill you." Because Beloved never experienced the wrath and degradation of slavery and of schoolteacher, and Sethe wasn't going to let her go back there. "Wasn't no way I'm gonna let him use you the way he used me. You my best thing." But Beloved is still in her baby's mind even though she's this grown woman. She doesn't understand. And Sethe believes that she can get her to understand. After Beloved comes back, she seems so affectionate and loving that Sethe thinks she's not even mad at her. After 18 years of being haunted by her in this house, Beloved (so Sethe thinks) now seems to understand why Sethe had to do what she did. And when Beloved finally says, "You left me," Sethe is dumbfounded by that and tells her, "You know why I did it." And Beloved says, "I don't know nothin'." But Sethe thinks: *We're all together now — you, Beloved, came back to be with me.* And she says to Beloved: "I'd give up every one of my tears just to take back one of yours."

But when she realizes that she's got Sethe, that Sethe would give her anything she wants — that is when Beloved decides to take Sethe out. Meanwhile the other daughter, Denver, wonders how this girl can come back in the house, wreak havoc, throw things, talk back, do whatever she wants to do, and Mama just sits there and lets her do it. But Sethe gives herself over to the loving, to her feeling of "I can't believe you came back to me and now I'm going to spend the rest of my life proving to you how much I love you."

"Love either is or isn't, Paul D. Thin love ain't

no love at all." That's what Sethe says. If you asked her to choose, there was no choice. That was the only thing for her to do. In her mind there was no other way. There was no sense of should I or should I not. That's why it was done with such resolution. She was never out of her mind when she killed her baby. It was her intention to take them all to the other side.

Paul D's comment to Sethe that it's "dangerous to love any one thing that much. Best thing is to love everything just a little bit" is really a slave's view of love. Because there you have no right to yourself. If you don't belong to yourself, then anything that anybody chooses to do with you is okay. But when you fully own yourself, you stand up for yourself against anyone who would stand against you. Sethe only owned herself and could do what she did because of the 28 days of freedom that she experienced. Perhaps there's a different mentality when all you've known is slavery; then you may choose to adjust in your mind to slavery's conditions. But once you've known freedom and true life you never will allow yourself to go back. Once Sethe could own herself and therefore claim her children and know that they were hers to love, nobody was going to take that back.

There was an article I read in *The New York Times Magazine* a while ago about slavery in Mauritania today, and the reporter said to one of the slave women, "Have you been sexually abused? Have you

been raped?" And after hours of trying to communicate this idea to her, the woman said, "Oh, you mean the men who come at night?" And when I talked to this reporter she told me that the concept of rape is inconceivable when you don't own your own body. The women didn't believe that their bodies even belonged to them, so they didn't feel a sense of violation. Which is also the way I feel about Sethe and her fighting for her children; because once you own yourself, you can't let anyone violate you.

The miracle of this—and I don't know if I can get this message across to every African-American descended from slaves—is that you can come from that heritage and *still be here.* If you can come from that kind of legacy of strength and courage, there is nothing greater than that. And it should be celebrated every day. That's why I was never satisfied with Black History Month. Even though I know there used to be a time when there was no acknowledgment at all. Many people labored to first get a Negro History Day which over the years progressed to Negro History Week. And now Black History Month. I was always resentful of it being reduced to a 30-second public service announcement about Harriet Tubman and a few others. And this became clear to me during the making of BELOVED. I understood why it feels so condescending. Because we are a people who have helped to create the entire country having lived our lives day by day—giving our services and ourselves, carrying the strength of our Ancestors. The Ancestors being the bridge to this moment. And it's totally patronizing trying to chronicle that giant legacy in one month. Black History is American History and should be treated with the same regard and woven into the tapestry of American lives.

It's not about material accomplishments (though we have plenty of heroes and sheroes who have excelled against all odds). It's about the courage and strength over time which means the power it took to stand and remain a people in a world that denied you free will. Denied your humanity. This is what should be exalted. And that includes all the great-grandmothers and -fathers whose names would never *merit* a history book but whose determination and inner will keeps us standing.

I had to think about what it took to be Sethe, and I came out of it with the greatest sense of pride—pride I never even imagined. What would it take to live on a plantation where you can't read . . . the newspapers around you don't

tell you anything about you . . . you don't see anything . . . hear anything . . . or know anything that says that your life has any value? Nothing. Not a poem, not a book, not a song. And the songs that exist are about God—Just let me get through, We can make it over, Hold on to God's unchanging hand—that's what gospel came out of, the need for something to hold on to, a belief that something is bigger than yourself. So what would it take to have the kind of spirit and will to say, *I am better than this*? I don't know if I would have had that, the will to take my children and to run and not know where I'm going, to say: "I'm going to go North—but which way is that? Freedom is North, which way is that? I don't know how long it's going to take me to get there and I don't have shoes to run, or food, or know whether there will be water along the way, but I know I'm better than this."

I think that ultimately what BELOVED *says* is that the past matters only to the extent that it makes you who you are today, to the extent that you use it to create what you have today. You know, every person who has come before you existed for this moment that you're in now. You're part of your past, and the past lives with you. It can benefit you today. You carry the strength and power and courage of the Ancestors with you every day. And that's what every one of their lives was for: so that your existence might be possible. They were a bridge for you to get to this moment. And that is what I want to share with every African-American—don't let slavery embitter you but let it truly free you, because you have been through and survived the worst. So, my God, look at what you can do now. You have all that behind you.

In the film, during the scene where Sethe describes her milk being forcibly taken from her by two young boys at Sweet Home, I did this scene for every woman whose milk was ever stolen—whether it was the milk that was stolen or the mo-

ment she was degraded and embarrassed and humiliated and taken down. I did this scene for every one of them. All the people who make up

the lives before me, every black person who ever struggled, every prayer ever uttered, every song ever sung—every single one who struggled so life could be better, who knew they were the seed of the free—we exist because of them.

We don't need to live our lives in bitterness and anger now, consumed by hatred and fear because of what happened then. Now we truly are liberated to create the highest vision for our lives that is possible. Each of us, no matter who we are, but particularly those of us who are descendants of slaves, is living the vision the Ancestors had for us and for themselves. We are the manifestation of their vision. And we have an obligation and responsibility to carry that on. It should be the foundation of strength and peace and courage and honor and reverence. That's what the legacy of slavery can mean for us today.

I collect slave memorabilia and have ownership papers from various plantations listing the names and prices of the slaves. I brought one of these to my trailer on set. And I would literally call out the names—Joe and Bess and Sara and Emily and Sue and Dara—from that list every morning. I lit a candle, spoke their names, and attempted to honor their spirits. It's not just me, Oprah Winfrey, playing Sethe based upon what I created in my mind from the book and the questions I asked myself about Sethe. For me a characterization doesn't begin in the pages, it begins on the day the character is born; so in trying to create the person that Sethe was—where she would have come from and what her past would have been—I tried to bring all of that with me to the role.

You not only use your body and your physical self (this is how I see acting) but you also use everything that comes before you to create the interior life. So I would try to focus myself, and to enter that space, that part of myself that I know is connected to the things that are bigger and beyond and behind me.

I was striving to create a life that, in ways you cannot articulate, will be felt in the spirit of the character. I ask my body to be the carrier for the spirits of those who have come before me in a way that is most meaningful to the character that I have created called Sethe. That's the goal: never to put yourself in the position where you're acting—just be there, moment to moment, not falling into the trap of letting yourself act by asking yourself, "How should I do this?" Just become the vehicle for that history, that truth, that character.

When I was preparing for the role of Sethe, I read an article in *Smithsonian Magazine* about a man who had done a trek a year previously, starting from Kentucky and taking himself all the way to Canada, shipping himself in a box from one state to the next. He wrote about his experience, and I had him on my show and asked him to create a day so that I could feel what it would be like to go through that journey. So he took me into the woods, blindfolded me, sat me on a bench under a tree, and said, "We're going to regress you." I told him that I was too strong-willed to be hypnotized. And he said, "Just try to let yourself go with it." So we did this whole regression process. We started in 1997 and tried to push back the memories from that year, went back through the decades until he said to me, "Now we're in 1861. And when the blindfold is taken off, everyone you see will be representative of that period. Your name is Rebecca, and your story is that you live in Baltimore as a free woman. You were captured overnight and brought to this place. Men broke into your home, they brought you here, and now this is where you live. And just like every other slave, it's up to you to take from this what you believe to be true of yourself and let go of that which you think is not."

I sat blindfolded for a very long time, and then I heard the hooves of a horse and smelled the alcohol on the breath of a man who came up to me. Apparently, he was playing the role of a slavemaster and he asked me who I was. "Rebecca," I said. "Where are you from?" "I'm a schoolteacher in Baltimore with three children, and now there's been this horrible mistake." "You're a nigger gal," he said. "Doesn't matter to me what kind of school you teach in. You're one of those smart niggers, ain't you?" I was blindfolded and couldn't see him and I replied, "No, no, I think you don't understand." And that's when he said to me, "You don't think nothing, gal," and went on to tell me that some woman who ran the place was going to come to me and if I learned to obey her, maybe he and I could get along and I could come and visit him sometime in the big house—that whole sexual stuff. Then he left.

I heard the horse leave and sat there for a long, long time, just trying to take in what he had said. The idea that slavery prohibited your thinking and your *ability* to *act* on your thoughts penetrated me in a way I had never perceived. I started to weep uncontrollably. Then another woman came—a black woman—and

told me who she was on the plantation. She worked in the big house, and these were the rules. "But you don't understand, I'm a free woman," I said. "No, no, you don't understand, child, you ain't free no more, you belong to Mr. So-and-so, just like all of us do." Then she left and I sat there for another long period of time, crying.

Probably more than anything else, this experience helped me get into my role for BELOVED, for I would remember every day what it was like crying under the tree, absolutely hysterical, saying to myself: *I know I'm Oprah Winfrey, I know that's who I am, let's just take the blindfold off, this is making me nauseated, sick.* I felt an indescribable pain. Then I'd say to myself: *Try to calm yourself, think of what it feels like.* And what it felt like was death with no salvation. And that became my definition of slavery:

Death with no salvation on a daily basis. Darkness with no hope. Just pretending to live. And I also remember thinking: *I couldn't feel this if I didn't know what freedom was.* I went to the

place inside myself that knew what freedom was like and was then told that I no longer had it. That was my biggest connection to understanding why Sethe did what she did. She just knew that she refused to be a slave. And the experience I had didn't leave me bitter, it left me with the greatest sense of light and hope. Because I knew I'd been there: I came from there, from that hole of nothingness in a world where every moment told you that you were less than nothing.

You know, just in their everyday lives I think there are a lot of people who are enslaved in their own minds. And to a certain extent I was, too, and that's what growth and evolution are all about—getting to the point where you experience the essence of yourself, of your freedom, of the freedom that the universe has given you to be all that you can. Everybody is at a different level of experiencing that; I refer to it as different vibration levels. It's where you are. I think that for most people today, they can choose to be "slaves." The difference between that and the previous enslavement of black people in this country is that we didn't have the right to choose then. Every other human being makes that choice for him- or herself—to be or not to be. As long as somebody doesn't have the foot on your neck, you can change your way of thinking about anything. What slavery did was take away your ability to think. And thinking doesn't matter if you can't act on the thought.

One day I was thinking about Sethe and about the last words of the film, which are spoken by Paul D to Sethe—"You your best thing"—and I recognized, in a way I hadn't before, that was my motto for life. And it's the message I try to carry to everybody on my television show everyday. All the work that I do is for people to see that for themselves—"You your best thing." It's not what your boss thinks of you, it's not what your mother did, not what your past says about you. Every day you have the right to choose for yourself the best for yourself, regardless of what your life circumstances are. You can choose to feel differently about your poverty, your discrimination, about the way you've been treated because *you are your best thing.*

And this is also what is reflected back to me. There isn't a day in my life when somebody doesn't tell me, "You've changed my life." Of the 15,000 letters I get each week, many of

them say that to me. And I used to just hear the people say, "Hi-Oprah-you-changed-my-life," but recently I decided to live in the moment and not just to discard these as simple greetings from well-wishers. So I started saying, "Really? How did I? Tell me, what did I do?" Somebody would say, "I was watching your show and decided I was going to go back to school." Or, "I was watching your show and I used to beat my kids and thought that was the only way to do it, and now I've decided maybe I just might try talking to them. It certainly takes longer and it's a lot harder but I have a better relationship now with my children."

I believe that intention rules the world. We have the world we have because each of us intended it to be this way. So there is the individual intention and the collective intention, and that works on every single level. I believe all of our thoughts and behaviors come first from intention—which causes things to happen and the resulting effect always follows. What one puts out comes back, in every single instant of everybody's life. Whether you're aware of that or not, physical laws exist; but beneath the surface of every physical law there is also the metaphysical. My original intention in making BELOVED was that people would be able to feel deeply on a very personal level what it meant to be a slave, what slavery did to a people, and also to be liberated by that knowledge. That was the purest of my intentions, but not the only one.

My intention and goal since I was a young girl has been to do the best and be the best I can in every moment. Fame and fortune was not my goal. I just wanted to do the best I could in every single instance of my life. And I made that decision in the third grade in Miss Driver's class. I turned in my first book report (it was on a book called *Honestly Katy John*), and I turned it in early. She had such a fabulous reaction to it (and to the fact that I had gotten it in early) that I decided that I was always going to turn in my book reports early and that I would go beyond whatever limits were set for me. "Oh, you want it Wednesday. I'll have it by Monday." That kind of thing. And I remember having that concept of

how to rule my life in the third grade.

Most people are unaware of their intentions; they live subconsciously. I try on an everyday basis to live consciously and to be aware of my intentions, not just of my actions. That is how I live my life.

I always ask myself (and others I work with), "What is my (and your) intention? And is the intention pure enough to carry you through the difficult times so that you never waver?" Trying to make BELOVED over the past 10 years, sometimes the timing wasn't right, the director didn't seem right, or the script wasn't in the right condition. But I always knew, though I didn't know when, that everything would line up to create the best possible film. I've never felt so joyful as when I was working on BELOVED. The only other time I've experienced this joy and challenge was during the making of *The Color Purple*. And during that time I felt, how could I top that dream! Then this happened. So now I've decided I'll stop dreaming. I'll just leave myself open to whatever the universe has to offer. Because God can dream a bigger dream for you than you can dream for yourself.

Oprah Winfrey

THE
JOURNEY

or

AN *almost* DAILY KEPT ACCOUNT

of my thoughts
and impressions

while making the movie

called

BELOVED

THE
JOURNEY

or

AN *almost* DAILY KEPT ACCOUNT

of my thoughts
and impressions

while making the movie

called

BELOVED

PART TWO.

Called Kate [Forte, head of Harpo Films], after speaking with Jonathan Demme. He's coming to dinner Thursday, January 9, to discuss the possibility of directing BELOVED. Kate said, "Dare we hope that life can be this good?" I dare hope. ¶BELOVED. Could this be that after 9 years BELOVED is moving forward? Nine years of unwavering faith, but not being able to interest studios? Could this be?

WEDNESDAY, JANUARY 8, 1997

Holy God! Jonathan Demme is coming to dinner. What
kind of plates should I use? I have two sets of plates. Should I use the white plates or the ones with the design in the middle? I think I should get new plates. Where shall we eat? Shall we eat in the dining room or the breakfast room? No, let's make it casual. Okay, let's serve seafood. Maybe he's allergic to seafood. Maybe we should check.

THURSDAY, JANUARY 9, 1997

MORNING: I can't concentrate. The fact that Jonathan Demme's coming to dinner means he must really like the script, otherwise he wouldn't be coming. Right? EVENING: Unbelievable. When Jonathan and Ed [producer Ed Saxon] went out of the room for a moment, Kate and I were jumping up and down and dancing like three-year-olds. He [Jonathan] really likes it and says he can't wait to see me play Sethe. He didn't say yes, but I think "yes" is coming. Unbelievable. I think this finally could happen.

Arrived in Philadelphia still reeling from the Mad Cow deposition. [In January 1997, Oprah was sued for maligning beef.] Crew cut, Southern, young snuff-spittin' lawyer, asking me if I'd just use my "common sense." Humiliating. They loved it. "They took my milk," just like in *Beloved*. It's a slimy business. I'll use it for a higher good. First time I ever felt pinned down, my back against the wall. Looking into the eyes of those lawyers, I felt like when those mossy-toothed boys had Sethe pinned down in the barn. ¶That's maybe what Maya [Angelou] means by saying, "Thank you." Even in that moment there was something to carry away and be thankful for. The ability to use it now. I should focus and celebrate that I'm in Philly to *finally* make the movie of my dreams, but I can't shake the demeaning, gut-wrenching deposition.

But, I will!

7:00 A.M. pickup. Had to shower at Kate's because I couldn't get my hot water to work. Got to the trailer, and saw the wigs. They're extraordinary! I've never in

my life seen anything like the work that must have gone into them to make it look like Negro hair. Extraordinary. They rolled 3 strands at a time in a spindle, boiled them to break down the texture, then baked them. Magnificent work. I like the disposition and countenance of Ellie [Winslow], the makeup artist; Alan [D'Angerio], the hairstylist; Peter [Owen] the fantastic wigmaker. ¶It was an extraordinary day. Hard to take it all in. When I first saw Jonathan, my heart soared. Skipped a little beat. He's so engaging—buoyant, enthusiastic. I almost feel shy around him. His love is so encompassing, I don't know

how to hold it, take it, feel it. Could it be this lovely, lovely, dear man thinks as much of me as he says he does? I don't know how to take that in. Still. ¶And so here I am, just trying to absorb it all. I want to feel every moment. ¶Today we did screen tests. No one mentioned anything to me, but I think my weight is okay. I'm still not where I need to be. Losing 5 pounds more by next week would be delightful. Can I do it without making myself crazy? ¶I had some weepy realization moments— 10 years ago I bought this book. A dream has come true. We're going to be remembering history, and creating some, too.

¶Beah Richards [who plays Baby Suggs] said today: "We're on assignment. The Ancestors have called this one up. It's so strong. So strong." I believe her. She also said the same thoughts I was thinking while rereading *Beloved*. How did we do this? Survive and remain sane. She said, "I know why nobody talked about it." Yes, I said, like survivors of the Holocaust. There are no words.

¶The tree went on my back [prosthetic scars that represent the whippings by the mossy-toothed boys]. I wept. Could not, but tried to stop myself. Couldn't. There's a tree on my back. Felt it. I pray to be able to trust to go all the way there. To feel the depth, power of what it all means. Today was emotional but I stopped myself from moving deeper. ¶I'm already so connected to the story that standing with my back to the camera for the test, I couldn't stop myself from tearing. I wasn't even trying to. The feelings just took over. ¶I know it's all there. May I be able to reach it in its fullest abundance on the days I need it most.

I pray for the Ancestors to come.

I awakened early, and did my daily prayer to the Ancestors.
Then I ran to gym. Went to Hagley Museum to learn to cook as they did in the 1800s. Practiced making biscuits and pies, shelling peas, cleaning greens, slicing bacon, grating salt and sugar, and cooking on a nineteenth-century stove. My heavens how exhausting. A woman's work really was never done. Gettin' the kindlin', lighting the stove, going out to the pump to wash the greens. The work it took to do the simplest things. ¶Came back to the hotel to learn that my Florida home is on the front page of another tabloid. More notably, my toilet is on the front page. One of the workers took pictures and sold them. You know you're famous when you're not on the cover but your toilet is. ¶Yes, betrayed again, but now I feel not so vandalized—just used.

One incredible day.

We did a read-through with almost all the actors present.

Sitting around a table, not in costume; Jonathan asked us not to act, just read the words. And just the words took us to another place. I had trouble finishing my last scene with Danny [Glover]—"You your best thing"—he was tearing and I was about to lose it. When we finished, there weren't many dry eyes in the room. We realized what an incredible journey this is we're undertaking. ¶Then spent 2 hours having

a new "tree" placed on my back. This is a modified, more interpretive tree. Three hours standing up straight as they applied it, branch by branch.

It's hard for people to understand struggle without violence. But it really is not the way. Violence only begets violence. You can hang all the guilty people in the world and nothing will change. But you kill a Martin Luther King, Jr., and the signs that said "White" and "Colored" come down. I'm so grateful to have had the opportunity to lock horns with Baby Suggs. She is what love is all about. And love helps you look at the hostility and weep if you will and laugh when you can. Beah Richards (BABY SUGGS)

[In order to research her role, Oprah participated in a re-enactment of the Underground Railroad. In costume, with a new identity, she literally escapes from a plantation; and endures running and hiding to avoid capture. It was grueling, painful, and authentic.]

The Underground Railroad experience allowed me to go inside to feel the grief of losing control of your destiny. The meditation process to transition from 1997 to 1861, being blindfolded and vulnerable, having no power over when you can even speak. Amazing. Amazing Grace. Look at where I come from. Look at where I am. My God from Zion! It's incredible. The realization of the depth and Truth of it. Slavery was about having no power whatsoever. That's what became so real to me yesterday. More than a concept of no freedom. Freedom, I felt with such clarity, is the ability to think your own thoughts and do with them what you will. Choice. ¶I briefly glimpsed the reality of

NO choice. It was deadening. It was so painful. I didn't want to feel it. Not even in that controlled, contrived space. So deep. So real. So much pain.

¶I'm trying to define Sethe, but it's hard to focus on particulars. I feel that I already know her in my spirit. Reading slave narratives. *Bullwhip Days*; *Roll, Jordan, Roll*; the autobiography of Frederick Douglass—Beloved, Beloved, **Be loved.** The Underground Railroad experience was invaluable—helped me touch the place that was so real and painful—to experience and know the loss of free will. I understand fully now why Sethe killed her children. For her that was the only choice. To know the sorrow and desperation of not having control of your being, your destiny. To know your thoughts don't matter— you can't act on them. Loss of free will. Loss of dignity. Loss of self. A living death.

I saw Sethe's house on Bluestone Road for the first time today. Stopped me cold.

¶Kristi Zea [production designer] had sent me blueprints and sketches but I wasn't prepared for the leap my heart took when I set eyes upon it. I thought I was back home in Mississippi at the house I was born in, looking out over the road that had no name. Everything about Sethe's house—the slant of the land it sits on, the outhouse, chicken coop, clothesline, even the stump in the front yard—reminds me of my grandmother Hattie Mae's home, the home I was raised in for the first 6 years of my life.

¶I couldn't help touching everything—the rocker on the porch—and remembering being afraid and climbing into my grandmother's lap during a lightning storm, and her saying, "Be still. God's doing his work." There is a peach tree planted on the side of Sethe's house. In Mississippi, ours was a fig tree. I walked inside Sethe's kitchen; seeing all the jars of canned pickles, okra, and corn lined up on the shelf. I remembered canning all day with my grandmother in the kitchen and hearing the lids pop. The fireplace with the hearth where we sometimes cooked. It's Sethe's home. My home.

Memories. Rememories. History. Creativity. Life.

We rolled the first film today. It was an extraordinary moment, surreal. I knew it was happening, but I couldn't believe that it really was. Ten years of waiting, wanting, and the realization that this is what the waiting has come to. Again, hard to take it all in. Trying not to be too dramatic about it. Trying to accept the moment for what it is. But it is a bit overwhelming. ¶I've had an easy day of running through the chamomile fields. What an appropriate way to begin! I told Jonathan, I always wanted to be a woman with a basket running through a field. I thought it would be a field of flowers but I'll take chamomile. ¶Tomorrow is the first day of dialogue. Am I ready? I think so. I bring the force and grace of history and pain with me, carrying the Ancestors in my heart, hoping, but also knowing, they, too, carry me. I've been paid for. "Your crown has already been purchased," Toni says. "Now put it on your head and wear it." I ask God for grace, and the power of the spirits whose lives went unnoticed, demeaned and diminished by slavery. Calling on you. Calling on you. I try to prepare in terms of logic, reasoning, what would she be thinking— chronologically— but I really believe I can call her up. Her and so many others. I'm counting on them.

Was nervous—anxious—trying to find Sethe's voice. Today we filmed the first speaking scene: "Paul D, is that you?" I'm too Southern. Afraid to let my own voice come through. Afraid it's too Oprah-like. Recognizable, familiar. I've got to move away from that idea. ¶I was so caught up in the day I forgot about channeling. ¶Spent the morning kicking off my shoes, washing my feet. ¶It was awkward in the beginning trying to feel our own way, and develop a connection between the

characters. One of my clearest directions on this day: Jonathan kept saying to me, "Look into his eyes, you keep looking away." I think I'm embarrassed— staring directly into a person's eyes with this kind of meaning. At first it felt as if we were just saying words. It got better by this evening—many takes later. ¶It's an awesome challenge: Using yourself but losing yourself. All day Danny and I didn't speak on camera a full 10 minutes. Tomorrow will be better. We're finding our way.

It was better indeed. We're finding the rhythm. "On our way to something special," Danny says. He is brilliant in this movie. Facial expressions, thought process, mannerisms. He will make me better as an actress. "Devil's confusion, Sethe. Makes me look good long as I feel bad." His smile erupts and embraces the screen. Saw dailies today— the "film" is beautiful. Not impressed with the sound of my voice for the first day's work. I truly was trying to find my voice.

people. When Kevin Ladson [the prop master] was anxiously repairing Danny's knapsack, all eyes were on him, waiting. Even though he was holding up the shot, Jonathan generously thanked him when he was done and the shot continued. ¶Today, a little 5-year-old extra named Ray Ray was upset about wearing his wig. He was hot and bothered. Midafternoon, I saw Jonathan personally go get the child some orange juice and take it to him. ¶My close-up's tomorrow. ¶I

Moving across to the pump, washing chamomile—that felt truthful. ¶So impressed with Jonathan and his grace, his love and generosity of all

strive for Truth—to release myself and let Sethe take control. To be in the moment is truly the only quest. And to let that moment live its own Truth.

When I was making this film I tried to think of my grandparents, who were born in the 1890s, which meant that their parents were born around the time Denver was born. When I used to sit around with my grandparents I was dealing with well over a hundred years of experience, because I was dealing with their parents as well. So I inherited their energy and emotional presence—the way in which they walked, ate, revered their Maker—all of that I saw

There are no words to describe this. The film. Danny's first words. When I ask, "Paul D, is that you?" and he responds, "What's left." Oh, my God! He spoke for all who've come before. He's the bridge we've crossed over on. It's historic. It's grand. It's blessed. It's Beloved. ¶The power and depths of what I feel is too much to write down in one place. In practical terms, I was pleased with myself, my performance. I in no way measure up to Danny right now. He makes me better. Makes me want to stretch to get "there" sooner in every moment. ¶It was an extraordinary day. Cloudless. No humidity. Close-ups from my angle. Jonathan at

first gave me so many instructions my head was spinning: "Let's see the flash of anger in Sethe. A look that conveys 'Who's coming in my yard?' She's got to protect Denver! Think adrenaline. Listen to Paul D. You're anticipating his answers. Really ask the question 'How long has it been?' as though you don't know the answer. Do something totally different with the knowledge that Baby Suggs is dead. Really feel her death, what the death of Beah [Richards] would mean to all of us." ¶So many directions means, yes, you're as bad as you think you are. Talk about Insecurity. I'm majoring in it today. I'm nowhere close to the Truth. Channel. Channel. Don't be afraid.

as a kid, all of that I sat with as a child. And that experience was transferred to me, not in words, but in smell and taste. And I call on these things. I've tried to call on them and invoke them, too. My own ancestors—and everything I got from them, even subliminally—are here for this moment of my life. Because the story of Beloved is not just about a few individuals, it's also a collective story; it's a collective journey. **Danny Glover** (PAUL D)

This thought came while making coffee:

I am a descendant of slaves. I came from nothing. No power. No money. Not even my thoughts were my own. I had no free will. No voice. Now, I have the freedom, power, and will to speak to millions every day—having come from nowhere. I would be a fool to give up the *Oprah Winfrey Show*. I must figure out a way to make it work. To surround myself with people who are enthusiastic, who want to do it, who are not burned out, who understand the worth of this extraordinary time and opportunity to change people for the better.

The morning was abuzz with talk of a meeting

in my trailer. Word was we needed a conference about me looking "too pretty." This is a first! In all my days I never have been called "too pretty" or expected this to be a subject of discussion. My teeth are too white. I'm too "luminescent." I need more sweat. All gathered in my trailer for discussion: J.D., Kristi Zea, Ellie Winslow, Colleen Atwood [costume designer], Kate, Tak Fujimoto [cinematographer], me. Me who grew up feeling I was anything but pretty. So I better be smart. Held a full discussion about it today with all these people present. Lord, it is a new day. ¶Saw yesterday's dailies—it translated on-screen better than I was feeling at the time I was doing it. I remember the first 2 weeks of *The Color Purple*. I felt exactly this way. Can I do this? Am I good enough? ¶Every day my confidence grows, and my respect for Jonathan knows no bounds. I see him getting orange juice for extras— giving a thumbs-up after every shot—a wink, a "very good, very good." He's a wonder.

One extraordinary week? A note from Jonathan to all departments, dated July 3, 1997.


```
TO:       Dearly Beloveds in
          ALL DEPARTMENTS
FROM:     Jonathan
RE:       Thank you

Thank you everyone who made our
extraordinary sets and locations
come together so superbly in every
way. And in such record-breaking, .
back-breaking time.

Thank you everyone on the crew and
in the cast and in every single area
of this production for creating the
greatest first eight days of footage
I've ever seen.

Love, Jonathan
```


Wow! I want to be more like that, acknowledging and showing appreciation to everyone for their contributions to my life and work. He makes you want to open your heart a little wider, that Jonathan.

¶Thinking more and more about how to take the remaining 2 years of the *Oprah* show, and turn them into something special with enhanced leadership. ¶We worked only 4 days this week, and shot Scene 19 from every angle possible, even the ghost's point of view. "Thought you said she died soft." "That's not Baby Suggs." "Who then?"

Paul D's main motivation and concern is his overriding love for Sethe. After wandering for 18 years he has come, in a sense, to be saved, but paradoxically he ends up being a savior, too. I don't believe that coming into Sethe's house and living with the ghost is disturbing to Paul D, considering what he's been through—the

¶Danny Glover is brilliant. His performance is the finest display of truth coming to life I have ever seen. I, on the other hand, am still trying to find my way with this character. I know who she is but I'm too sympathetic to her condition. Instead of letting her iron-willed self come through, I've been empathizing. Let go and Let God take over. That's my mantra for the rest of this film.

journey he's been on, everything he's seen. Sethe reminds him of the women he's met along the way, women who have lost their brothers, their fathers, their husbands. So he is willing to embrace this place as somewhere he wants to stay, some place to plant roots. He feels that he doesn't have to wander anymore. Danny Glover

I light my candles to the Ancestors, but must rely on the Higher Authority to take me there.

¶**My biggest scene this week.** "I've got a tree on my back and a haint in my house and nothing in between but the daughter I'm holding in my arms." I gave at least 3 impassioned deliveries. I could tell each time HE [Jonathan] wasn't moved. After the first 2, he asked that I make her less embracing of Denver. More steely. After 3rd take, he said, "You're still not giving me the cold, 'I can't believe this girl is going off again in my house' Sethe." Kimberly was screaming so loud—I was afraid of not being heard and having to loop all of that—and was struggling to keep her quiet and under control. So the scene became more about keeping her from losing it, which brought the truth to the moment and elevated it from being a "nobody knows the trouble I've seen" speech. I took the sermon quality away and made it Sethe's "Declaration of Independence." All because Jonathan kept pushing me to go farther. I wasn't sure how I could do it, because I had played it over in my head for 10 years. Couldn't remove myself. Jonathan said, "It's too predictable, you're making it a speech," and I started to get scared because I realized it had been a speech in my head for years. So I went into a corner and silenced myself, released that fear, and said, "If y'all are coming, come now." Then I went back in and nailed it. The next day I got a note from Jonathan saying: "You slayed me."

¶Kimberly cried, amped out. Her performance went all the way. Truth. She did it over and over. So many times I forgot to

count. Magnificent. Jonathan said he felt privileged to be a part of that scene. That you're drawn in it—overflowing.

¶The camera was on Danny for the "they took my milk" scene. I couldn't stop crying. God help me when it's my turn—my close-up. May I do this scene in tribute and in truth to every woman whose milk was stolen. Whose body was taken. Whose soul and spirit were ravaged. Whose pride was shattered. Whose dignity was lost. Whose self was controlled. "They stole my milk. Come in there and take it. That's what they come in there for."

So my turn came (my close-ups) and came and came. The milk scene. What JD does is have you abandon what you thought was the way to do a scene. My concern and panic was for crying on camera, on cue, in close-up. Pressure. My fear of crying on camera was reminiscent of 13 years ago on the set of *The Color Purple*—

only this time I didn't cry when I could have cried. After the first take, which I managed to sob by the "taking of milk" line, JD asked that I be less sympathetic to Sethe. (JD did not want me to cry—

and this time I could have wept buckets.) And he said I was having too much empathy for Mrs. Garner. "Her eyes rolled out tears," I remember. He instructed me to tell the story matter-of-factly. Wait until Paul D takes your breasts before crying. I thought it best to tell the story and pause during certain points. "I went into the barn looking for Halle, and that's when schoolteacher saw me, and came in after me with his boys." JD thought the straight telling—no pauses—was a better choice.

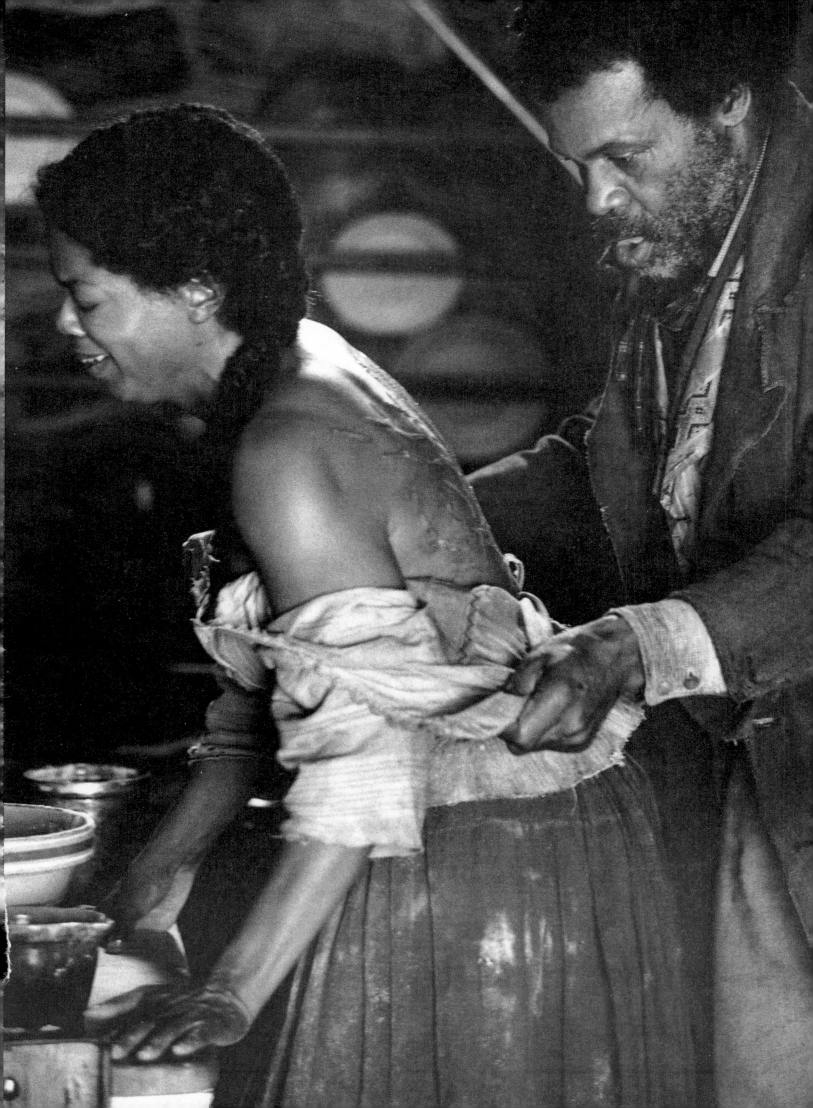

¶I listened to music— something instrumental about dreams that made me sad, put me in a sad place. Could not for all the wealth I possess cry on cue. I tried giving myself over to Sethe. I thought of all women who've had their milk taken, who needed a man's arms to fall into. I thought of every ancestor as a Bridge to me in this life. Looked at the pictures from Bullwhip Days. *Sometimes I could get to that state and hold it, but I could not cry on cue. The anticipation of the moment would jam me up. Hard to tell that story unemotionally,*

and then take 3 beats and be emotional. I felt like I failed—Jonathan, the Book, myself—but I'm moving on. The dailies were powerful even though there weren't enough tears. Perhaps if I were better trained I could have done it. ¶And then I remembered, in The Color Purple, Adolph Caesar saying, "Give yourself over to the character. Let the character take control. If the character wants to cry, she will." I realized Sethe did not want to cry in the scene, at that particular moment. ¶But I literally gave it my best. I was grateful for the response in dailies. People applauded.

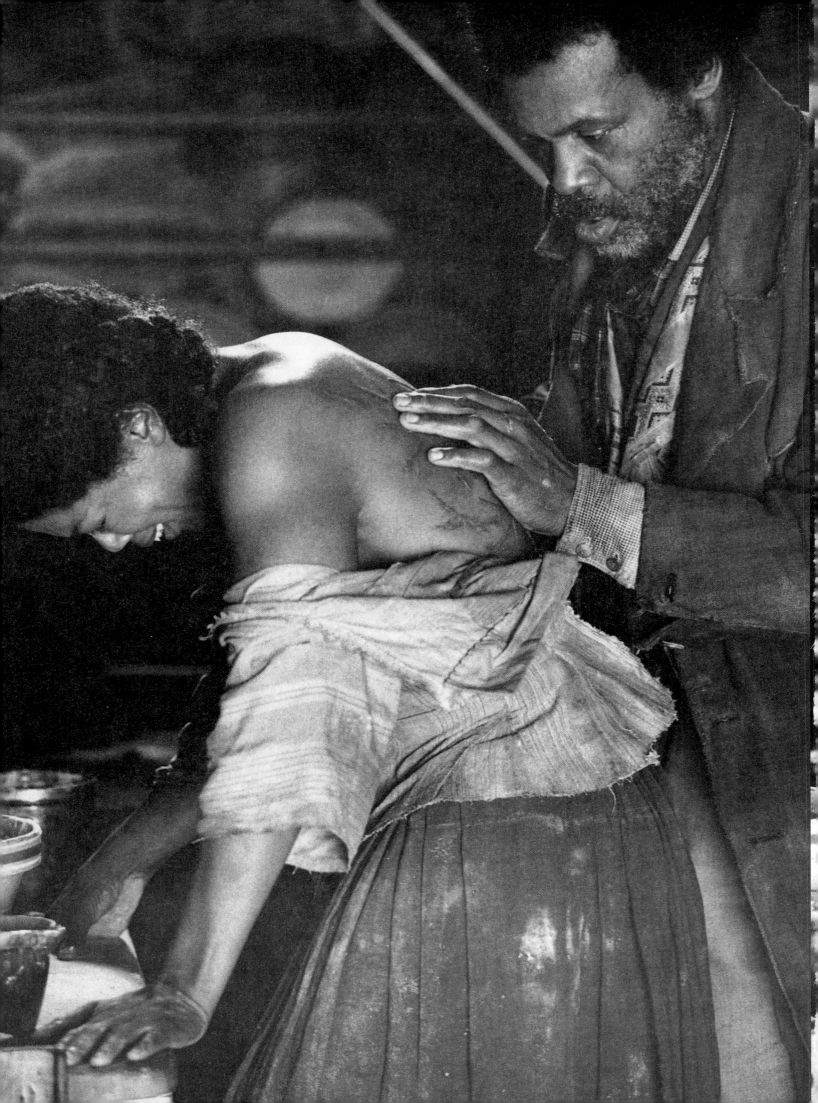

Today I've never felt sicker. I was having the "tree" put on my back, and was overcome with a wave of nausea. Then I had a chill, then . . . diarrhea. But I willed myself to get through it even though there were moments, half lying on the table, when I thought not. JD came in and told me to go home. Him telling me to go home—the thought of rearranging production on my account willed me better. And in a hurry!

¶ **I'm so glad I stayed.**
Beloved's arrival was worth the day.
Thandie Newton—Brilliant! Brilliant!
and Beyond. Channeling at its finest.
¶Beloved's arrival brought a surge to
the room, to the cast, to the movie.
Complete and total abandonment of
self—Thandie has something I'm striving for and only feel moments of
achievement. Beloved breathing. Labored,
wheezing. Beloved taking her first bite
of food. **Brilliant**. ¶The simpler the
scene, the more complex for me. How
do you do nothing? How do you eat
at a table or glance across a room?

My mom is from Zimbabwe, and when I was born they named me Thandie, which means "beloved" in Zulu. And it
wasn't until after I started working on the film that someone reminded me of that. Perhaps I didn't think of it
because I didn't want to imagine that this was something that was fated. If I dwelled on the magnitude of it, it would
be too overwhelming. Someone once said to me that once your work doesn't seem scary to you, then you should give
it up. There always has to be a certain amount of awe for what you're doing.   **Thandie Newton (BELOVED)**

¶I am terribly insecure about my acting—it's not something I do often enough to know I do well. Jonathan has been so helpful and encouraging, every day, every scene. When Sethe is looking at Beloved's shoes in the doorway and says, "Denver, is she feverish?" JD tells me, "Really look at the shoes." He says my nuances are terrific. He says I have a gift. I'm not certain. But I'm grateful he believes I do. ¶At the end of this week, we watched Beloved breathe and be fed in dailies. The scene—"you like shortenin' bread"—featured beautiful Kimberly's bold eyes and tentative excitement. Jonathan hugged me and said many times over, "Thank you for this wondrous experience." AMEN.

I would describe Denver as lonely, sad, insecure, angry, lacking in and searching for love, proud, determined, loyal, devoted, compassionate, and sensitive. She's a very special girl, and there are so many levels to her, so many challenges to her life, with all the internal struggles, the worldly struggles, and the household struggles she has to deal with, overcoming them to become a beautiful woman with a future. She's a great American character, and she's the first multidimensional character I've ever played. **Kimberly Elise** (DENVER)

Today I did the scene where Denver says, "I think the baby ain't gone. I think Baby Ghost's got plans." Never really got the scene. Jonathan asked, "What are you thinking when she says that; your reaction needs to be more complex." I panicked a little inside 'cause I think I can't or won't be able to do what he's asking. I never did what I thought I should have, even though I asked for extra takes. He said, "I'm thrilled to hear that," when I requested the takes. I could tell he wasn't really happy, but settled a little on my account. ¶I said today to Kate and Ed Saxon that I have such respect and admiration for JD that if the worst were to happen—if he were to throw me out of this movie—

I would understand and still love him. I now pray that I won't have to prove it. ¶Still not there. Haven't had the pivotal "click" scene where I turned over everything to the character and it worked. I'm praying.¶Tomorrow, I have to film love scenes with Danny. ¶Today, I had to have a much-dreaded conversation with JD about my breasts. I don't want to see them on camera. I saw storyboard drawings of Sethe in bed after lovemaking with Paul D, her breasts sitting straight up. "Jonathan," I said, "when I lay down, my breasts do the same. If you want them to stay up then we need a breast stand-in." "That's all right," he said, "the scene isn't about breasts, we'll work around them." Thank the Lord in heaven.

My first love scene with Danny. Oh, I was a wreck this morning. At dress rehearsal with Danny, we walked up the stairs, breathing as one, having just fought the baby ghost. Jonathan had a talk with me alone in the hallway about my anxiety over the love scene. He said these kinds of scenes are difficult enough to do. The crew is anxious, everyone is sensitive, and it is my role, not only to relax, but to help everyone else do the same. "Kissing is a wonderful thing," he says. "So relax and enjoy it." Which only made me more of a wreck. Then Danny says to me, as they are resetting lights, he's never done a stage kiss before. Ah, I think, neither have I. Then I realize—after he says, "No, I do the real thing"—what he means. Oh boy, what's worse than a wreck, because that's what I turned into. I asked Donna [a dresser] to please get me some lemons to suck on. I hear lemons give you fresh breath. ¶By the end of the day, I'd surprised myself. After my initial fears, and the first take, I was able to let Sethe take over. And she had a great time! Can't wait to do it again. ¶Sucked a pound of lemons today.

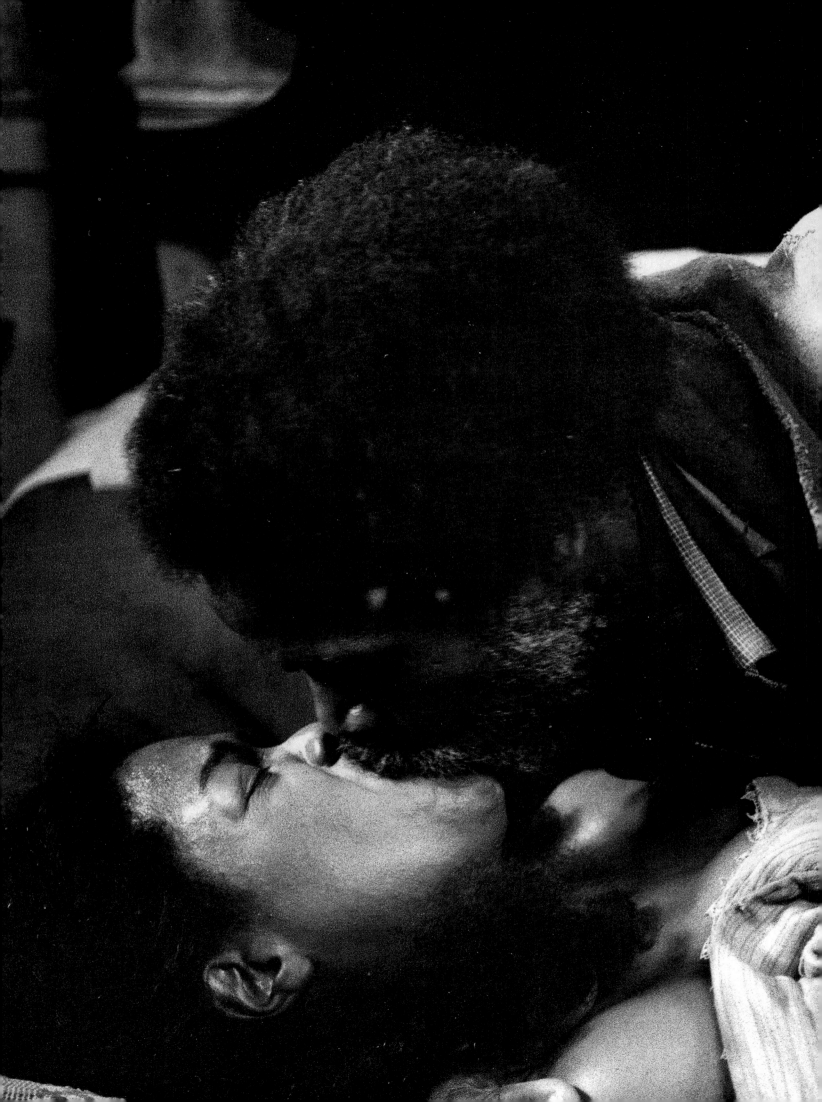

¶Came home to discover Versace was murdered. Who would have imagined that? The world seems out of control. Who's next? How bizarre, scary.

Beloved asks: "Where your diamonds?" Sethe tells her mother story: "Mark the mark on me. Mark me, too." Did this scene all day long. So many takes, I lost myself in them. Having to re-visit Sethe's mother being hung and restrain myself from being emotional in the telling. I had to give up all of my preconceived notions about this speech regarding Sethe's mother and tell it as though it was the first time it ever hit my brain. I was able to let Sethe take over but it took some work. I'm exhausted from the telling. I could see that bit in Sethe's mother's mouth every time. Her hanging from the tree. I'm exhausted from the telling.

There's a saying in our culture: Don't take notes, take note. That is, remember. So the culture became our remembered selves. And there were among the survivors of the journey of the Middle Passage those women who had the ability to remember, who had the ability to go into trance and seek both past and future. They were the key to the survival of the people over here because they remembered enough not to be hopeless, not to think we were going to be erased. We had no voice, we were branded, and nothing was left but our memory.　Beah Richards

Saw the dailies from "Where your diamonds?" and "Mother" speech. At the time, Jonathan wanted me to do it faster. I wasn't sure it would work. He's right again. I whispered to Kate while watching myself on-screen, "Do you think my lips are too shiny?" She said, "No, I think they match your shiny face." We both started cracking up. She was right: my whole face was glistening. They're overcompensating with the sweaty, oily look. ¶It being Friday after an intense week, we had champagne. One glass and we were hysterically laughing throughout dailies. Having fun—a good, ole time—with all of us. I love this whole group.

I'm mortified and holding my breath. JD just called and wants to come over and talk to me. On a Sunday! It's so serious he's coming to my hotel on his day off. Word has it it's about dailies, but it could be— of all mortifying things—weight. ¶**So he came, sat down, and said, "I want to talk to you about dailies.** On Friday, you kept saying faster, faster, and faster. I want to know why you were doing that? Were you trying to send me a veiled message?" The question stunned me a bit. I had to really think: Why? My answer was I wanted to get to the take where he had requested me to go faster, delivering the lines more matter-of-factly— and see how different that would be. While watching the previous takes, it still seemed too slow. It was my way of acknowledging that I realized I still hadn't done what he'd asked me to do. And, wanted to hurry to the take where I took to his direction. Evidently, it was disturbing to him. It disrupted the important reason for dailies. ¶**It was like having the principal come over to your house and talk to you personally.** My God, this has never happened to me in my whole life. For a moment, I felt like I was 7 and going to cry. My friend Gayle [King] said, "My God,

I've never known you to get bawled out." ¶**Thank God it wasn't about weight.** What a relief! But if this doesn't whip me into shape, nothing will. 'Cause God, God save me from the weight-disappointment talk. I remember the mortifying potato chip moment: when I opened the car door leaving JD's house last May, there, right on the car seat, were bags of chips—that weren't mine! Mortifying. He was so alarmed he had to call me about it. ¶**I've learned some tremendous lessons.** First of all, JD coming to see me personally and dealing with what he perceived to be a problem head-on is what I need to apply to my own life. Also, I learned about having respect for myself and acknowledging for myself what a great take it was and not blowing it off. And, knowing that you can tell a person the truth and if it's a true relationship, you become better from it. And respect them for it. ¶**JD was right on every level—** I shouldn't have been making jokes, making light of any part of dailies. It's the opportunity that everyone, especially the director, has to look at their work. I was not mindful of that. Had I not had a whole glass of champagne before entering dailies, I would have been more sensitive—not to mention, I probably wouldn't have felt "loose" enough to be so frivolous.

Today started out with me writing an apology note to Jonathan. "Thank you for our talk. You were right. I was wrong. You are the best. Thank you for making me better." I felt like a heel, but I wanted Jonathan not to feel a bit uneasy and know how totally accepting I was of his criticism. ¶Today's great direction note: "Instead of looking away [when Paul D speaks of a witless woman who was hanged for stealing ducks she believes to be her children], look more deeply." ¶Tomorrow we film from Danny's point of view. He's looking at *me*. My reaction to hearing the news about Halle: He witnessed Sethe being violated by schoolteacher's boys, and did nothing about it. "They took my milk." Plenty of feelings there. Today it felt as natural as rain. Everything clicked! I always choke at close-ups and I'm so relaxed and effortless in other shots. Aren't actors supposed to love close-ups?! I don't. Why is that?

The Yin and Yang of life. I'm thinking I finally hit a rhythm, got Sethe going in the right direction. I'm praying for the spirit of Truth to enter the scene. I'm releasing myself. Letting "them" come. Thanking them for coming. ¶Then Toni Morrison arrived, and watched dailies. Afterward, she merely asked, "Why were you so angry there?" I couldn't answer. I immediately went to self-doubt, thinking that she hated my performance. I'm thinking, *She must be disappointed. It's not the way she intended, the way she wrote it. I'm disappointing her.* My single greatest disappointment of the movie. Devastating. Then I also learned about her one note to Jonathan: "Oprah Winfrey is emotional, Sethe is not." ¶I guess I was just feeling too good about the day, about life. I came to work ecstatic to be there. Rolled down my windows to say to the woman carrying groceries, "That sure is a pretty dress, ma'am." Made her smile. I came in waving to the depressed-looking daily officer opening the gate. Made him smile. I was feeling great about Scene 99. People applauded after the first take. But Toni rekindled all my fears about doing justice to Sethe: her arrogance, her knotted, private, walk-on-water life. So, I will continue to learn from this and get better.

JD knew I was affected by Toni's question. So he came to my trailer to see how I was handling it. He left with tears in his eyes, saying he was bummed that I was so bummed. Seeing him so affected deeply affected me, and I tried to release all of my self-doubt. The fact that he believed in me so. That was the moment I absolutely fell in love with Jonathan! ¶I'm trying to get over my self-doubts. I must understand that JD is right: whatever I'm doing, right or wrong, I must remember that a movie is a movie, and a book is something different.

Jonathan said tonight that this has been the most productive and fulfilling week of his film career. He never had a week like this one, he said. Can you imagine JD feeling this way? He's had 25 years doing this. This is my second feature film. And I feel the same way. ¶We started the week filming Beloved's angle of choking on a raisin. By Monday night we had filmed Danny talking of Halle in the barn (the scene that almost wasn't). Tuesday was my "Loft? What loft?" reaction: "He was there. How do you know? He saw those boys doing that and let them keep on breathing?" The scene clicked. It was effortless. ¶I went home and my bones ached all night. Had to get up in the middle of the night and take aspirin. The next day when I told Danny about my bones, he told me his bones had been aching, too. He needed acupuncture. He said, "We took the journey, baby. We went all the way there."

¶We ended the week with Paul D in the tub, naked. What a body! If Michelangelo had seen Danny's body, he'd have said forget David, let's use Danny! Kate calls his butt "the high and the mighty."

The time is approaching. I'm beginning to feel real pressure about the decision to continue or not continue the show. Just read from *Even the Stars Look Lonesome*, Maya Angelou's book. Here's the reason to continue:

"*We were stolen and sold from the African continent together. We crouched together in the barracoons, without enough air to share between us. We lay, back to belly, in the filthy hatches of slaveships in one another's excrement, menstrual blood and urine. We were hosed down and oiled to give sheen to our skin, then stood on the auction blocks and were sold together. ¶We rose before sunrise from the cold ground, were driven into the cane field and the cotton field together. We each took the lash that pulled the skin from our backs. Each of us singled out for the sexual enjoyment and exploitation of those who desired our bodies but hated us.*

. . . We may yet survive our grotesque history."

¶So this is where I've come from. How dare I even think of quitting. Now I have a voice that can be heard around the world. I must find a way to say what needs to be heard. May the Ancestors and all the power that is God abide with me. Direct my path. I am not afraid.

¶All day—all weekend—I've been counting the hours to get to the set on Monday and do the "28 Days of Freedom" scene. I'm open to all the possibilities it can bring. I'm trying to let go of all the preconceptions. Let me take the words, the space, the history, the moment—and let them carry me. Come on, Sethe. Counting the hours: 8 hours and 45 minutes before pick up. Can hardly wait for the great exploration of process.

I failed in the close-up of the "28 Days of Freedom" scene. Four takes. Before the last 2 takes (medium shot), I said to Kate that I need to open myself up. Felt like I was behind a wall and couldn't *break* through. I was just stuck and couldn't come unglued. So after 4 takes, Jonathan decided to move the camera around on Danny. I felt that was the right thing to do. Although I knew it meant I had not succeeded in channeling and nailing Sethe to the wall in the speech of my dreams. But that's exactly what it had become—a speech. The words were so poignant that I allowed myself to get attached to the *words* instead of throwing them away, making them real and spontaneous. ¶I fell in love with the words: "Twenty-eight days—twenty-eight good days of freedom—and on the twenty-ninth day it was over." Jonathan said my delivery was "great for the Literary Guild, or for books on tape," but not for Sethe. ¶Channel. Channel. Channel. Where are you, Sethe?

I finally got it, though I was afraid. Afraid of the previous day's failure. Afraid of being "locked in." Fourth take, I got it by giving Sethe room to breathe. As Sethe says, "I woke up in the morning, decided for myself what to do with the day." I decided to ad-lib. My problem is, and has been, feeling that I have to remain so true to the words of the book. Jonathan says, "Your preparation is excellent. But you're being harnessed by the book." ¶I used to walk around with the book, constantly referring to it. Now I've finally let it go.

I was having some difficulty with the fireplace scene—Sethe with Beloved and Denver. I was afraid of "acting." How do I express feelings of unconditional love for a returned ghostly daughter and make it real? I had such anxiety about making it right. Jonathan picked up on it and asked me the next morning, "Are you okay? Are you having personal problems? I noticed you were really anxious in that scene yesterday." ¶This was a revelatory scene for me. I realized I had no place to go to conjure up feelings of the unconditional love a mother has for her daughter. I couldn't fathom what that would feel like. Sethe tucks in her daughters—the simplest of acts. JD commented that I was handling the pillows like rocks. He said, "you know what it feels like to be tucked in by your mother." I realized: I have never had that experience. And never imagined it until this moment. Pretty amazing.

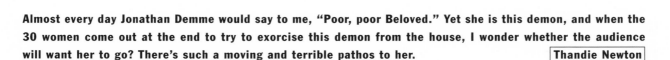

Almost every day Jonathan Demme would say to me, "Poor, poor Beloved." Yet she is this demon, and when the 30 women come out at the end to try to exorcise this demon from the house, I wonder whether the audience will want her to go? There's such a moving and terrible pathos to her. Thandie Newton

I thought I had the best role in the film, but it was just my arrogance. Beloved and Denver take this thing to another level! Today we filmed the scene where Denver asks,

"Why you call yourself Beloved?"

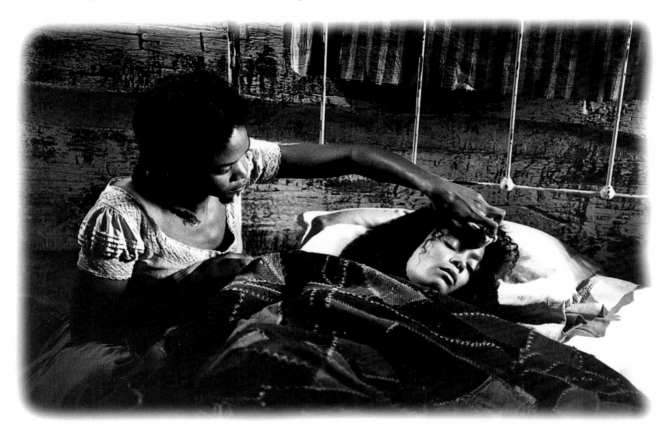

Amazing transcendence! It was exciting to watch these two actors in dailies. We were all in awe of what they brought to the words.

This past week was spent fighting a ghost on a shaky set. [special effects, mechanical moving set that enabled floor boards to move and furniture to fly across the room] Not very interesting work—more about tables and stools flying. Stop. Wait. Emote. ¶We filmed the "Carnival" scene today. Amazing production design! Hundreds of extras

meticulously and authentically dressed. Such detail. Wendy [Graham, Stedman's

daughter], Gayle and her children were all extras. ¶I had a pep talk with myself.

I was starting to feel gloomy about having only three weeks left. I decided

sadness, in this case, is a choice. So I choose to celebrate each day instead.

I'm amazed that I'm on the cover of *Life* magazine with a title that says I'm the most powerful person. How'd that happen? Feels like someone else.

MONDAY, AUGUST 18, 1997

I needed to go to Chicago to have a meeting with my staff to focus on the new season. We're going to be in trouble: We're out of reruns. And I'm still here! I have to be here until mid-September. My staff is feeling pressure. I'm feeling pressure and torn. I so needed to focus only on this film, and now the reality of my dual life sets in. ¶JD heard about my plans to go to Chicago on my *one* day off, and had a conversation with me which kept me in Philadelphia. Wise decision. He thought Chicago would change my focus and zap my energy. He's so right. So, I had a conference call/pep talk with the staff instead. The gist being how do people lead their lives? How can we help them do it better? In every aspect of their lives, how can we lead them to their truth? First we must be led to our own. Who are *we*? What do *we* stand for? What do *we* believe? How can what we say be an influence for the good, the better? ¶All of this so-called "power" means nothing if we don't share it. Use it for the good. How do we do that? That is the only question to be answered. The shows will follow that answer.

There are no words to describe my feeling of overwhelming pride at having the Divine guidance and wisdom to listen and feel that this movie could be what it has become. ¶Watching Beloved emerge from the stream. Watching Paul D and Beloved do the "Touch me on the inside part and call me my name" scene. Bless me. Bless me. May all the angels caress me. I am proud of me. I am proud of every one of us who made this happen . . .

Jonathan is my hero. He eliminated exposition from a scene and it turns out to be one of the best scenes I've ever done. He cut the fat, leaving just the essence. Sethe's sons are gone! What's to come?

¶During the scene where we come into the room and see Here Boy [the dog] flying all over [because of the baby ghost's interference], instead of feeling shock or surprise, Jonathan tells me to feel only sadness.

Princess Diana is dead.

Killed in a car crash. Suddenly, of course. Unexpectedly. She "woke up in the morning and decided what to do with the day," and went to Paris, never expecting it to be her last time. No one would have imagined this. I'm stunned. Thinking about her. Her life force. What her life has meant to all of us. A Princess, literally, living in a castle but just struggling to be more human—like we all are. Now the struggle is over. I feel such sadness. What does this mean? What does this mean? I know we say you never know the day, the hour, but who is really prepared for this?! Doesn't feel real.

Haunted. Can't shake Diana's death. Trying to figure out what it means to me and the rest of the world. What did she come to show us? What are we supposed to get from this untimely death? Take nothing for granted. Even a Princess living in a castle can hit a wall. ¶I pray to have no fear to move forward and do what needs to be done. To do it for the great Glory and Honor of my creator. ¶So, I'm starting this week to "take myself down": physically, emotionally, spiritually. To go to the place one needs to go to create the last scene of BELOVED. The "30 women" scene is coming up. ¶Wrestling with my fears of dying, and not being prepared. I need to take the time to redo my will. Get my house in order. Diana's death has shown me it is irresponsible to live otherwise. As the Bible says,"Be ye also ready." I feel changed by this death of a Princess. I feel there is no time to waste. And, I need to turn up the throttle . . . *and live more intensely.*

Fun day. Lots of energy . . . the kind that comes when you haven't been eating a lot. Montage scene. Twirling, twirling around the house with ribbons. Terrific. And so much fun. I was giddy.

Second day of "30 women" scene. Lost my voice. Went all the way there in the wide master shot. How can I do that every time? I still haven't mastered it by the medium shot. Today, I was spent. ¶The dolly grip operator said, "You're on the news this morning. They say you're quitting your show." That's odd! Who told them? He said, "They say it's a reliable source." ¶Funny how putting on a corset and bloomers can totally remove you from the hype of the world. I'm just barefoot on Bluestone Road. Haven't turned on a TV, or read a newspaper. Feels like another world. ¶I hear it's the buzz—I'm quitting! Before I started this movie I felt strongly that I could end the show. I've surprised myself with the revelation to go on and see what the end will be. Now I believe this movie and the preparation for this movie has given me the strength and insight to continue. Strange how I thought, and so many others around me thought, this experience would make me want to do more movies. I know, and I think all of us feel, that a movie and experience like this one is a gift. You're blessed to get one in a lifetime.

Hitting the ball out of the ballpark is what every take of Sethe going to attack Mr. Bodwin felt like. Wrenching, painful, sobbing every time it ended—no cameras rolling. Being healed—a laying on of hands. Amazing. Amazing Grace. For me it was my personal attack on slavery.

Jonathan just called. Gem of a man. Wanted to tell
me, "I'm so proud of you. Thank you for letting
us witness your ode to humanity in that scene."

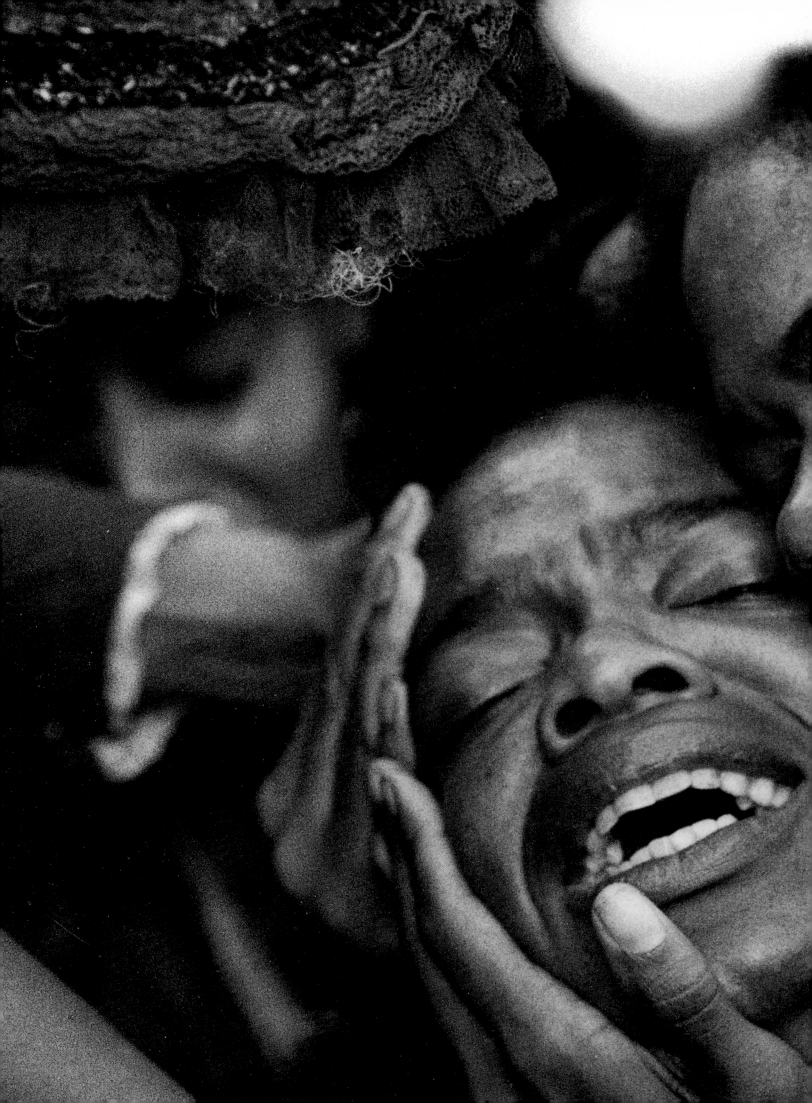

I have some pick-up shots to do.
I'm overwhelmed with emotion. I'm
full of joy, strength, courage, the
past, and rememories. It's a bitter-
sweet time. My final day of shooting
in the summer of my dreams. A
dream bigger than anything my heart
can ever hold. It will be a long time
before I can take it all in. I can honestly say I embraced every moment.
I did it my way. I have no regrets.

I conquered. ¶My greatest fear has been whether or not I could cry on cue. For the "Beloved left me. She's gone" scene, Jonathan freed me early on by saying, "You don't have to cry." He freed me, so I cried during almost every take. ¶I will never doubt Jesus again. ¶I went all the way there. "Follow the breath, and let the next breath be the one that may carry you out," JD whispered. Thank you, JD, and to all and myself who made *this* day possible. ¶I solidified my acting. One take after the next. I did it for those who were tired and had no voice to speak or be heard. I had a picture in my mind of a slave woman crossing the field from *Bullwhip Days*. I pictured, too, in a flash, Sethe representing the pain of all the lives. The sadness of having no free will. Determination, guts. The courage to run and just stand.

Home. Chicago. Done. Relieved. Happy. This part is done (except for the Winter scenes in December). The whole thing is so incredible. I dare not take it in all at once. Had a delightful time with Gary [Goetzman, a producer] and Jonathan last night and realized for the first time all the joy to come in the postproduction process.

¶Then we still will have the movie. So I feel not let down this time, as opposed to last month. Seeing Danny leave and thinking about his brilliant performance, what he has given this production, and what that will mean to all those who see it, just made me weep. I'm glad to be home. Alone. Glad to be Home.

Sunday. I spent the day resting. Worked out 20 minutes finally around 12:30 P.M. Napped all afternoon. ¶Dreaming Sethe dreams. Releasing her. Read an astonishing article today about a group of slaves living in Africa who know no rebellion. "God created me to be a slave just like he created a camel to be a camel." Will and desire are concepts of the free, the author says. So are making plans. "She had no plans." No concept of future. She and her children spend their days numbed by freedom.

¶As Baby Suggs says, "Let the children come." This is more than a movie. It's a heart beat, beat, beating on screen.

I can feel it.

We spent a summer creating BELOVED. It was the greatest gathering of *synergy, creativity,* and *passion*—where every single person who was involved in this project brought *everything* they had every single day. We all came together for this brief and *shining* moment called

BELOVED.

thank you, cast and crew

love Oprah

ABOUT THE AUTHOR

Oprah Winfrey plays the role of Sethe in the film BELOVED, *which she produced through her production studio, Harpo Entertainment Group. Harpo also produces prime-time specials, made-for-television movies, children's specials, as well as* The Oprah Winfrey Show. *Oprah first became interested in making a film of* Beloved *in 1987 when she read Toni Morrison's Pulitzer Prize–winning novel. Her participation in the film, directed by Jonathan Demme, is the result of her decade-long dream to bring this haunting story to the screen.*

ABOUT THE PHOTOGRAPHER

Ken Regan, founder of the photography agency Camera 5, has covered everything from rock'n'roll to the Olympics to wars in the Persian Gulf and Bosnia. He has photographed over 200 magazine covers and won numerous awards. Recently, Ken has been shooting unit and special photography on films such as Jonathan Demme's The Silence of the Lambs *and* Philadelphia, *Clint Eastwood's* The Bridges of Madison County, *Alan Pakula's* The Devil's Own, *Christopher Reeve's* In the Gloaming, *and Robert Redford's* The Horse Whisperer.